The Basic Essentials of
BICYCLE TOURING

by Mike Nicoson

Illustrations by
Mark Ingraham

ICS BOOKS, Inc.
Merrillville, Indiana

THE BASIC ESSENTIALS OF BICYCLE TOURING

DEDICATION

To my mom, Donelle Joy, for all of your love and support

ACKNOWLEDGEMENTS

Thanks to Sabine and David Coffee-Graf for reviewing the work and giving their valuable advice so freely. Thanks also to Dave, Dave Svetich for his help with the biophysiological/ athletic training parts of this book. I am indebted to Shelley Peffer and Celeste Staley for their comic support. Also deserving of credit are Ms. Mott & The Big Wazoo, Dave Cullen, Ja, Suzanne Smith, R. Randall Wilson Buisiness Services, Ignatius J. Reilly and all the medical staff at Club Fred. And a special thanks to my cover-person, Shannon McCully.

Published by:
ICS Books, Inc.
1370 E. 86th Place
Merrillville, IN 46410
800-541-7323

Library of Congress Cataloging-in-Publication Data

Nicoson, Mike.,

    The basic essentials of bicycle touring / by Mike Nicoson.

       p. cm. -- (The Essentials series)

    Includes index.

    ISBN 0-934802-73-4

    1. Outdoor recreation--Bicycle Touring.   I. Title.   II. Series.

GV1044.N53 1993

796.6'4--dc20   92-47123

                                                CIP

TABLE OF CONTENTS

1. CHOOSING A BICYCLE 1
Touring or Mountain?, Sizing a Frame, Rims,
Spokes and Tires, Gears and Derailleurs, Brakes,
Saddles, Handlebars

2. TOURING HARDWARE 11
Racks and Panniers, Bungee Cords, Fenders, Bottle
Cages, Trailers, Extras and Luxuries

3. ESSENTIALS FOR LIFE ON THE ROAD 17
Shelter, Sleeping Systems, Clothing: The Theory
of Layering, Riding Shorts, Footwear

4. GETTING GOING 23
Stretching, Care of Knees and Feet

5. ON THE ROAD 29
Basic Safety, Traffic Laws, Riding Skills, Cadence,
Shifting, Pedaling Techniques, Hills, How to Pack

6. GOOD EATIN' 37
Carbohydrates, Fats, Proteins, Vitamins and Minerals,
Water. A Touring Cyclist's Daily Needs, A Portable
Kitchen, Stoves on Wheels, Spoke Bending Recipes

7. PLANNING A TRIP 43
The Joy of Living on a Bicycle, Route Selection,
Where to Sleep?, The Shake-Down Ride

8. MAINTENANCE AND REPAIR 49
Regular Lubrication, How to Check for
Problems Before they are Problems, Repairs, Flats,
Out-of-True Rims, Broken Spokes, Brake
Adjustment and Pad Replacement, Broken Cables
and Chains, Tools

APPENDIX A 59
Equipment Check List

APPENDIX B 61
Mail Order Companies

APPENDIX C 63
Cycling Periodicals

APPENDIX D 65
Touring Guides

APPENDIX E 66
Repair Manuals

Index 67

1. CHOOSING A BICYCLE

So you want to go on a bicycle tour? Undoubtedly, your decision is a wise one. Cycling is fitness oriented, environmentally conscious and energy efficient. One of the least expensive, yet most enjoyable ways of taking a traveling vacation is by bicycle. There is simply no better way to drink in a landscape, to swim through and smell each field, each gurgling creek. If you spy a flower dipping gently in the breeze just stop and check its beauty. No need to pull off the road, find a place to park your 6,000 lb. behemoth, turn it off, literally unstrap yourself from its clutches, open the hatch, tumble out into a foreign environment and look at the flower. Just lean your bike on a tree and stroll on over.

The first thing to consider is just what sort of bike to use on your tour. Whether you are buying or just trying to figure which friend's bike you might borrow for the trip, one thing you'll want to concentrate on is the type of terrain you expect to be covering. Will you be riding over dirt or paved road? Be it on a bombproof mountain bike or a traditional, narrow tire touring bike, a multi-day tour will endure as one of your most cherished leisure memories.

For our purposes, let's assume that you will be mostly self contained for the trip. By this I mean that in some way or another (there is no right or wrong way) you'll be carrying a sleeping system and shelter appropriate for expected weather conditions, a limited amount of clothing, a cook set and stove of some sort, toiletries and any other personal items like cameras, books, games etc. If lugging around this much stuff seems like too much already don't be discouraged. In the following chapters I'll help you pare down your load to a minimum so that carrying all this will actually be a liberating experience. And if this style of touring still doesn't seem right for you, I'll recommend a few reputable outfitters who plan and transport all kinds of luxuries along a predetermined route— for a price. Whichever you choose, keep pumping!

Touring or Mountain?

If your route will be entirely on paved surfaces, it would probably save you quite a bit of energy if you used a touring bicycle. This looks like a typical "ten speed" with drop handlebars, narrow tires and a large cluster of sprockets on the rear wheel. (Figure 1-1) A touring bike is similar in appearance to a basic ten speed with the main difference being that the angles of the various adjoining tubes which make up the frame are a bit more obtuse. This serves to elongate the wheel base

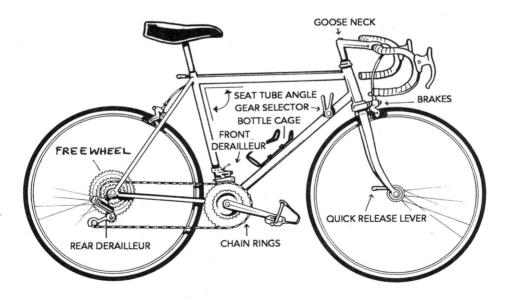

Figure 1-1 A typical touring bike is designed to travel over smooth surfaces at a high rate of speed.

giving a smoother, more fluid ride. Wider tube angles can be more easily appreciated after spending a few days in the saddle. The small gauge, high pressure tires commonly found on most touring bikes minimize resistance between you and the road surface. Likewise, this can be appreciated when pedaling a machine loaded down with food, shelter, clothes and a portable kitchen. So if the roads you'll be plying are paved, consider yourself well advised to use a touring bike.

If you plan on doing some off road riding along the way or, of course, if all of the planned route is going to be on dirt roads or trails then a sturdy mountain bike (Figure 1-2) is the choice for you. Mountain bikes (MBs) are built to negotiate rugged terrain. This means

Figure 1-2 A standard mountain bike is made to endure serious punishment.

they can take the added burden of riding over bumpy ground with the extra weight of all that equipment. In addition, a mountain bike retains the keen advantage of multiple gears (most MBs have 15-21 gears). However, the beefy frame means a much heavier hunk of metal to pedal around. And the wide knobby tires only add to the equation making for greater resistance between road and tire. You can compensate for this somewhat by increasing tire pressure, using tires with raised center ridges or by fitting your bike with perfectly smooth tires, called slicks.

Another option is a MB hybrid often referred to as a cyclo-cross. Originally developed for the harsh European winter racing circuit, this difficult to find crossbreed is fitted on a very light and strong frame with narrow, low profile knobbies. This type of bike would be ideal for dirt roads or trails which are in reasonably good shape. The higher priced MBs on the market today have many of the desirable characteristics of a cyclo-cross bike. So if long distance and hard riding are in your future you might consider spending the extra clams for a precision machine which will serve you well under even the most harsh conditions.

The most important thing to remember is that even your old klunker 3 speed that has been in the garage for the last decade or two, with a little work, can also do a fine job when it comes to touring relatively flat terrain. And the 1969 model Schwinn Varsity with two flat tires sitting next to it would get you through even the most demanding hill climbs, provided you get some new tires and devise a way to carry your gear. The point is that a typical tour for most of us (2-7 days) can be successfully accomplished with even the most meager machine. I once met a young Australian while at a campground during a tour along the California coast. He had just come from New York City— by bike! His bicycle, or "rail" as he called it, was a garage sale special. "Only ten dollars, mate. And that was with the rack." The rack, designed to tote textbooks, served to support a single canvas duffel bag tied down with rope. If he can cross the Rockies on a ten dollar bike, you have no need to buy an expensive rig for your first tour.

So if you already have a bike for the upcoming tour skip ahead to chapter two. If you are in the market for a new bicycle, the following points are things to consider before plunking down the cash to make sure the rail is right for you.

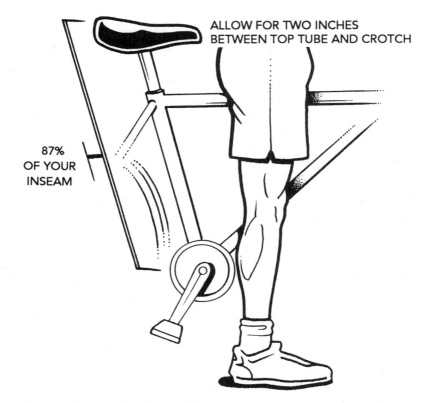

ALLOW FOR TWO INCHES
BETWEEN TOP TUBE AND CROTCH

87%
OF YOUR
INSEAM

Figure 1-3 Look for a comfortable straddle and appropriate seat tube length when
sizing a frame.

Sizing a Frame

Frames are measured by the length of their seat tubes in either
centimeters or inches. Look for a frame which you can straddle
comfortably while standing flatfooted on the ground with the top tube
just below your crotch. To custom fit the saddleheight, measure your
inseam while standing bare foot on a hard surface. Take 87% of this
number and adjust the saddle to this distance from the bottom bracket.
(Figure 1-3)

If it is within your power to choose your frame configuration then it
makes sense to apply a few simple rules when it comes to anatomy and
purpose. Taller folks with longer legs will most likely find that a frame
with a steep, or large seat tube angle feels best for them. While just the
inverse is true for people with shorter builds; they will pedal more
comfortably on a frame with a more gradual or smaller seat tube angle.

If you plan to be riding for an extended period of time or with an

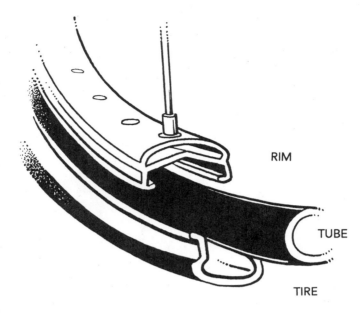

RIM

TUBE

TIRE

Figure 1-4 Clincher rims are durable and easy to work with.

especially heavy load then it will be easier on your body as well as the bike if you choose a frame configuration with a long wheel base. Most bikes that are sold as "touring models" should have an elongated wheel base. The reason for this is simply to distribute the weight over a greater surface area. This also gives one the feeling of a softer, more shock absorbing ride.

Rims, Spokes and Tires

Let's dispel a few popular myths. First, the smart touring cyclist today will choose clincher rims (Figure 1-4) for any type of riding on any kind of machine. Don't let anyone try to sell you on racing sew-ups. Second, a few years ago some people thought it a good idea to use tandem spoke arrangements for one person touring bikes. This meant that each wheel would have 40 spokes as opposed to the standard 36 thereby giving extra strength to the wheel and lessening the chance of snapping a spoke. Today's super strong alloys used in spoke manufacturing have made this once practical idea completely obsolete.

There are as many tire tread configurations out there as there are

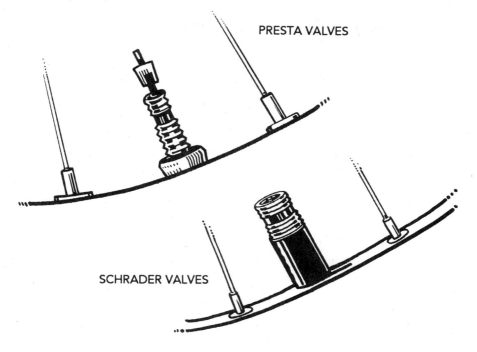

Figure 1-5 Schrader valves are much more common than Presta.

thick-thighed bike shop attendants. Just about any brand, even the least expensive, will get you through a month long tour nicely. If you will be riding a mountain bike on paved roads most of the day, but would like to do some off-road riding after camp has been set up, then choose a fairly narrow knobby tire (1.5 inches in width or less) with a raised center ridge for smooth pavement riding. Any configuration of low profile knobs on either side of the ridge will come in useful for dirt situations. If all of your miles on a mountain bike will be logged on the pavement then you may want to consider a set of "slicks". As the name implies, they are perfectly smooth tires wide enough to fit mountain bike rims.

Inner tubes of all sizes are fitted with two basic valves: Presta or Schrader (Figure 1-5). The latter are identical to an automobile's tire valve and this alone may be reason enough to fit your bike with this kind of tube. There are many more pumps out there designed to push air through Schrader valves than Prestas. This means being able to fill your tires at any gas station. Presta valves are usually touted as the "high performance" cyclist's choice although I don't know what is so

racy about not being able to find a presta pump attachment if your own
has been lost, broken or worse, permanently borrowed.

Gears and Derailleurs

If your route will be taking you over hills of any consequence you'll
want to seriously consider having at least ten gears. The gearing on a
bike is much the same as a car. Gears are simply a way of controlling
the ratio between the revolutions per minute, or rpm, of the motor (on a
bike read: your legs) and the rpm of the tire over the ground. The
derailleurs are the devices which change this ratio by moving the chain
onto bigger or smaller sprockets. Later we'll talk about how gears work
and how to use them efficiently. For now, just check to see that the
chain does not rub on anything when positioned on the farther inside
sprocket in front, called the chain wheels, and the far outside sprocket
in back, referred to as the cluster.

When shopping for multi-gear bikes these days you will encounter
two types of derailleurs, friction and indexed. Friction, which can be
thought of as an analog system, is the old style method of adjusting a
small lever to switch to the desired gear. Once you've found the gear in
question (you know you are there by feeling and listening) there is
oftentimes the need to finely adjust the lever in order to line the chain
up perfectly with the desired sprocket. With an index system, which is
more like a digital format, one simply clicks the lever and the derailleur
magically changes to the next gear and brings the chain into perfect
alignment automatically. In fact most index shifters have two levers,
one to move up through the gears and one to down shift. So which
system is best? Obviously the more complex index shifter has more
parts which means more of a chance for failures. Indexing also costs a
bit more, but even the purists agree that breakdowns are seldom and
the benefit of carefree shifting is worth the cost.

Brakes

Most road bikes are equipped with either center pull or side pull
pincher brakes. The difference, as far as we're concerned, is purely
academic. Mountain bikes are typically outfitted with center pull
brakes that have a great deal of leverage for extra braking power. These
are called cantilever brakes and they come in two styles, high and low
profile. It is recommended to look for the low profile cantilevers for
touring since they are less likely to interfere with panniers which will
be fitted very close to or right over the cantilevers themselves. This is

rarely a problem with road touring bikes since their brakes are low profile by nature.

Brake shoes, the rubber pads which come in contact with the rim, are mounted on calipers. Make sure that your calipers can accept more than one brand of brake shoe. Heavy loads tend to use up brake material at an accelerated rate. If you need new brake shoes along the way and can't find the super cool, space age brake shoes that the bike shop salesperson told you were essential for any serious touring, you will be inducted into the Fred Flintstone school of braking.

Saddles

The market is simply saturated with saddles. If you already have a comfortable saddle that is broken in to fit your buns just so then keep it. And make sure the shop keeps the saddle that came with the new bike and deducts the cost from the bottom line. Almost any saddle can be adapted to any post.

Some of the newer, higher price range saddles have pockets of gel in the seat to cushion your tushy. This may sound quite desirable and may even feel good at first but many experienced riders I know prefer a firm saddle to a gel filled one. No matter what kind of saddle you have, the first few minutes of the second day of riding will seem excruciatingly painful. Think of this as a short period of penance for all of the evenings you just sat in front of the television. The good news is that the pain will subside after the first ten minutes or so. The third day won't be nearly as bad. And after the fourth you'll be aching to get on the road and pedal through a fresh, clean morning.

Handlebars

Again there are as many different bar designs as there are bikers who dream them up. Some of the more popular configurations are drop bars, swept bars and flat bars for mountain bikes. Hunch over bars with elbow pads are comfortable for long distances but take some getting used to, especially if riding a loaded bike. Choose the type that feels most comfortable to you.

Getting a proper handlebar adjustment before you begin your tour can save you lots of neck and back ache later. Making a proper fit is actually a combination between saddle height and handlebar height. To see if the fit is right for you, put your elbow on the nose of the saddle with your forearm running parallel to the top tube. If the fit is a good one your fingertips will fall right on the handlebar.

2. TOURING HARDWARE

Now that you've decided on the right kind of bike for your touring purposes, it's time to discuss the matter of fitting your bike with the appropriate hardware which will turn a simple Sunday cruiser into a two wheel mobile home capable of supporting a life on the road almost indefinitely, and quite pleasantly at that! Mind you, none of the following methods of carrying your gear are better or worse than any others. All have their distinct advantages and deficits. It's important to find out which works best for YOU. Remember the Australian with the duffel bag roped onto a book carrier? That style of touring was perfect for him and he probably had an experience just as enjoyable and valid as the yuppie who spent $2,500 buying and outfitting his bike for the same tour. The only real essentials are a bike, a few free days and an imagination. But, as in all things, there are a few popular methods of arranging life on a bicycle and I would be remiss in my duties if I did not mention these practical, and not too expensive, ways of toting your worldlies.

Racks and Panniers

In order to simply carry your gear, which can weigh up to 40 lbs if going completely self-contained, you will need to provide some sort of rigid structural support upon which the weight will rest. The simplest solution is, of course, you. A small day pack can be stuffed with many of the items to get you through a short tour, providing weather is fair and you don't do any cooking. This can be quite fatiguing however and should only be seriously considered for shorter tours.

To make it easy on you let the bike carry the weight. The most common way of accomplishing this is by using racks fitted over the rear wheel, front wheel and over the handlebars (Figure 2-1). There are various brands of manufactured super-strong, super-light alloy racks to

Figure 2-1 Racks give structural support to luggage or panniers.

fit almost any bike, not to mention the inexpensive drug store models which work just as well for much less. From here you can devise an original way of bundling and strapping your gear to the racks or you can purchase special bags for this purpose.

Pannier is the French word for basket. In the cycling world the word refers to small bags which are attached by hooks and springs to the side of a rack. They are usually sold in pairs and are sized in cubic inches of carrying capacity ranging from 800-3,200 c.i. per pair. An extremely desirable quality of panniers is that they hang low on the frame keeping your center of gravity near the ground making for easy handling. While it is not necessary to buy a set of panniers, they do make packing and unpacking a hassle free process.

Bungee Cords

While panniers are excellent for keeping small articles together and on your bike some of the larger more unwieldy items, like your sleeping bag and pad (to be discussed in detail in chapter three) will probably need to be attached as single items. The simplest, fastest and most secure way of doing this is with bungee cords. Made of multiple rubber elastic strands gathered in a tubular nylon sheath and fitted with large, plastic coated hooks at either end, this simple invention will come to be your best friend after a few days on the road.

Another way to accomplish the same feat for less money is to cut old inner tubes into long strands 3/4 of an inch in width. A simple granny knot around any part of the frame or rack will hold quite securely due to the no slip properties of this type of rubber product. These bands are also very flexible and will easily stretch to twice their length. However, they will become brittle and snap if exposed to direct sunlight for prolonged periods.

Fenders

There are few things more annoying in our short lives than getting pelted with water and mud while riding. It is degrading, supremely aggravating and avoidable. Fortunately for us there are fenders which are made just to protect us from this sort of vehicular misery. You may never ride while it is raining, but you might enjoy cycling just after a downpour. There is no more intrinsically enjoyable time to whiz through a landscape, in my view, than when the leaves are still dripping and the air is brimming with that crackling newness only rain can deliver.

It should be easy to find inexpensive plastic fenders to fit your rail but don't feel that purchasing them is the only way to go. Fenders are also one of the easiest pieces of touring equipment to fabricate on your own. A long rectangular piece of cardboard clipped onto your rear rack with clothespins will serve the same purpose, although it will need to be replaced more often.

Bottle Cages

Stopping for a drink or a little bite to eat is not something you should have to do. Having a beverage bottle attached to your downtube or seat tube or both (Figure 2-2) will give you the freedom to drink while pumping along. Most bikes will either have a bottle cage or two small female fittings to accept the mounting bracket of one you purchase. If your bike has neither, you can buy strong plastic locking rings from any large hardware store. Use two of these to fix a bottle cage anywhere you like.

Figure 2-2   Who says touring isn't easy?

Many experienced tourists will have three or four cages on their bikes. These are used not only for beverages but typically to carry a fuel bottle for a small camp stove, which we'll talk more about in chapter 5. There is no limit to the things you can carry in a bottle cage. Try fruit, long packages of cookies, or even a can of mixed nuts.

Don't feel compelled to buy a cycling water bottle which can be quite expensive for what you are getting. Instead, buy a beverage at the grocery store in a plastic container that looks like it will fit in your cage. Metal cages can be bent to accept almost any size of container.

Trailers

If you choose to bring along large, bulky items which are not easily packed away in a pannier, like small children for instance, a trailer may be the perfect mode of baggage management for you (Figure 2-2). Don't be apprehensive about taking junior if s/he is too small to pedal him or herself. Many people have toured with children in this manner and found it wholly rewarding.

While two-wheeled trailers will add some resistance, keeping the tires fully inflated will help to minimize this drag. Most parents report that a book and a few small toys are more than enough to keep your young one occupied during the times s/he is not asleep or marveling at the ribbon of wondrous road unraveling before them at very close range.

If you're thinking about building your own trailer take a look at some of the trailers displayed in your local bike store to get some design ideas. Quality trailers are not cheap. If you have neither the expertise, tools nor the friends to make your own, you can always purchase one by mail order for less than retail. A list of reputable mail order firms from which you can procure a trailer is given in Appendix C.

Extras and Luxuries

Once you've devised a way to tote your gear (we'll talk about exactly what you'll need in chapter 3) there are a few superfluous and non-essential items to fit on your bike which, if you are into gadgets, could make your touring experience replete with technical bliss.

Keeping an eye on the passing miles is almost a logistical necessity for some people and the newest way to do this in micrometer style is to use a cycle computer. These tiny devices mount on the handlebars providing the rider with up to the second status of the day's ride, including speed, elapsed time, real time, distance, average speed, riding time, maximum speed and odometer.

If night riding is even a remote possibility you should arrange to have a headlight of some sort handy as well as side and rear reflectors. You can purchase a generator at a bike shop which will run off of your rear wheel. Or you can go the battery route. Either way a light source of some kind is a good thing to have handy.

Often times cyclists of different temperaments and riding styles will end up touring together. This is almost an unavoidable fact since no two riders are the same and even cyclists with very compatible riding styles may feel differently from day to day. Over the course of a day this can translate into significant distances between cyclists. A handy way to bridge that gap is with walkie-talkies. They can be especially helpful in emergency situations, when riders become separated in unfamiliar towns or in providing communication between lead and sweep riders in larger touring groups.

3. ESSENTIALS FOR LIFE ON THE ROAD

Having all you need to live quite comfortably for extended periods neatly strapped on your bicycle is one of the most liberating sensations available to modern humans. You can go anywhere there is food and water to be had, and you get there under your own steam. Below is an inventory of what you will need to be secure in creature comforts for any kind of weather.

Shelter

If there is any chance of encountering rain, high winds or extreme cold along your route it would be advisable to bring along a lightweight tent or at least a tarp to provide you with a modicum of protection.

A summer tourist pedaling through a relatively mild climate might get by very well with a large, lightweight, durable plastic tarp. Choose one with grommets and carry at least ten feet of nylon twine for each grommet to anchor the sides. To raise the center, take a small stone, approximately 1 inch in diameter, place it in the inside center of the tarp and wrap the tarp around it in the same way a Hershey's Kiss is wrapped only upside down. Now tie the end of a twenty foot section of nylon twine around the bottom to secure the stone anchor. Pass the line over a low branch, raise the roof and tie off (Figure 3-1). Keep the whole shelter relatively low and close to the ground to minimize the profile exposed to the wind. Always camp on the leeward side of ridges

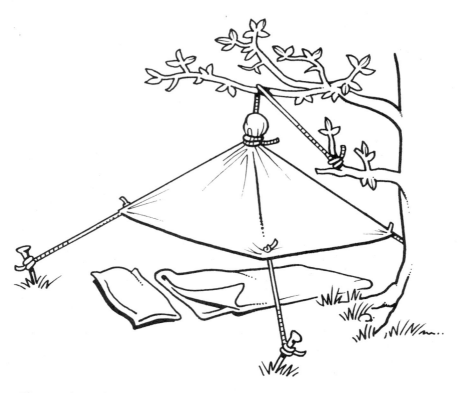

Figure 3-1 A mild weather shelter can be made from a tarp, a stone, and some cord.

and choose relatively high, flat ground on which to sleep.

Tents of numerous shapes and sizes can be purchased in any sporting goods store. A 3 season model will suffice for most cyclists. Make sure your model has a detachable rainfly, waterproof floor which extends at least 6 inches up the sides. A vestibule is a desirable feature since it allows you to keep gear dry without actually bringing it in the tent. If sharing a tent, make sure all parties know how to pitch and pack the tent in question before beginning the tour! And be sure to divide up the parts when riding so one person isn't stuck with carrying the whole thing.

Sleeping Systems

Slumbering outdoors after a full day of cycling, gazing upon winking stars through heavy eyelids is one of those transcendental experiences which is only surpassed by waking up in the early morning to a stunning array of colors in the east, then smiling for a moment in groggy wonderment and dozing back to sleep. But for the experience to be as warm and comfy as possible you need to give some forethought to your bed.

It is no longer a sound ecological practice to use live vegetation as your mattress. There are plenty of modern alternatives which are arguably more forgiving on a body than pine boughs. The most practical for our purposes are ensolite, or closed cell pads. There are also foam, or open cell pads but these breakdown easily and absorb water so they are better left at home. A combination of the two are the self-inflating pads commonly referred to by a popular brand name of Thermarest®. While these are the most comfortable of camping pads they do have an Achilles heel: if they sustain even the smallest puncture they are virtually worthless unless you can patch the leak.

To keep you warm through the night you will want an appropriate amount of insulation. This can be just a blanket for warmer conditions but if there is even a chance of it getting cold it is best to carry along a sleeping bag. Just about any sort of bag will keep you warm in temperatures as low as 40 degrees Fahrenheit. Bundle and tie it up as tightly as you can, or mash it into a stuff sack so as to be easily bungee-ed on the bike. Down sleeping bags are the best insulators for their weight but are also expensive. Synthetic or polyfil bags approach down in insulating powers but are heavier and bulkier. However, synthetic fill bags will keep you warm even when soaking wet while down is worthless once wet. To keep a down bag dry, place the stuffed bag in a plastic bag and close securely. Then place all this into a second, slightly larger stuff sack.

If packing ultra light you may consider a vapor barrier bag. Predicated on the fact that almost all of our outgoing body heat is contained in water vapor escaping through our pores, vapor barriers trap all of that warm, moist air next to your body. The key advantage of this system is space conservation since a typical vapor barrier bag can easily stuff down to the size of a half of a loaf of bread. You may feel a bit soggy in the morning but you'll quickly dry and so will the bag.

Clothing: The Theory of Layering

Unless you have arranged for a "sag wagon" to follow you with your wardrobe for the duration of the tour, it will be necessary to limit the amount of clothing you pack along on your ride. Therefore it is imperative that one be prepared for all kinds of weather with a minimum amount of apparel.

How do you adapt to the constantly changing conditions without having to stop and change clothes several times along the way?

Start by wearing light, breathable material next to your skin in order to wick away perspiration. A short sleeve cotton tee-shirt and lycra biking shorts are a good first layer. Over this wear a thin insulating layer. A long sleeve polypropylene shirt and pants work well since they have great insulating power and will also keep perspiration away from the body. A polypropylene top and bottom can eliminate the need for bulky cotton sweatshirts and fleece jackets. Donning a wool cap and some gloves may also be a good idea. If it is very cold (below freezing) you may need to put on a second or third insulating layer depending on how low the mercury dips. Remember that you will be cycling which will generate quite a bit of body heat in itself so don't over do it.

Your last and outermost layer should be a thin wind and waterproof shell. Gortex is an excellent product since it allows water vapor to escape but is impervious to liquid water. If gortex is a little pricy for your budget, get some light nylon wind pants and a windbreaker and treat them with Scotch Guard. This should keep you dry and warm in all but the most demanding conditions. (Figure 3-2)

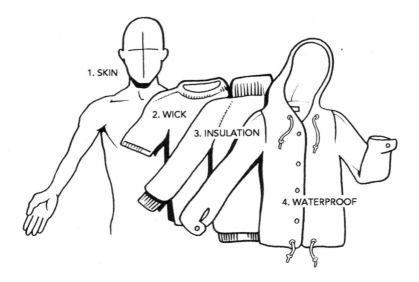

Figure 3-2 A layering system like this one can keep you warm, dry and adaptable.

As both you and the ambient temperature warm up throughout the morning, stop for a moment, peel off a layer and stuff it back in your bag. If it is wet or very foggy out, you may just shed layers of insulation and keep the outer shell to keep you dry. Indeed research has shown that people can remain warm even in a snow storm with only a thin, waterproof shell as long as they are working at a moderate pace to produce body heat.

By noon you are at the valley floor and have peeled down to your original layer of shorts and a t-shirt. You've just pulled out of a small town when you notice a large thunderhead building a few miles ahead. This is a good reason to always keep your shell layer handy at the top of your pack since you never know when you will need it in a hurry.

Riding Shorts

While it is true that before the lycra craze men and women toured countless miles in regular shorts or even pants, it is also true that the newer, lightweight lycra riding shorts hold many key advantages which a first time tourist will appreciate. Two selling points are the padded crotch/seat area and the no-chafe material.

Virgin buns will undoubtedly be sore the first few days of a tour. But padding in the crotch and seat will help to minimize this discomfort and enable you to cycle more comfortably for longer stretches. Secondly, the characteristics of lycra insure against chafing. Tight fitting and very slick, this fabric will allow your legs to move freely over the sides of the saddle without causing painful skin abrasion which can easily occur when one pumps at about 4,800 revolutions per hour. If you feel immodest about wearing such a tight fitting garment in public you can simply wear a second pair of loose fitting shorts over the lycra active wear.

Footwear

Although there are plenty of cyclists in this world who bike long distances with heavy loads on just bare feet and no pedals at all, just the spindle part, I'm certain that given the choice they would prefer to use the whole pedal and a sturdy shoe. So should you.

If one considers the way in which power is transferred from your leg to the crank arm (Figure 3-3) it is evident that a great deal of force must traverse the length of your foot to get to where it will turn the crank. Pedaling with a soft soled shoe can not only be fatiguing but injurious as well. For this reason cycling with a solid sole is a good idea because

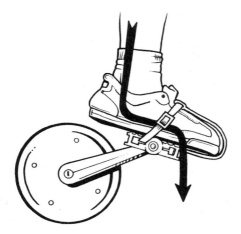

Figure 3-3 A sturdy soled shoe can help to carry much of the force from leg to
pedal.

it will carry the force which your legs are transferring to the pedals,
saving your foot considerable strain.

Toe clips are useful for keeping your feet in good position on the
pedal without any effort on your part (Figure 3-4). They also allow you
to pull up on a pedal while simultaneously pushing down on the other
for extra power. There is no cause to feel trapped in toe clips since most
have straps which can be adjusted to fit loosely around the foot in order
to accommodate easy entry and exit.

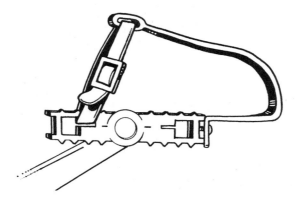

Figure 3-4 A toe clip keeps your foot in the optimum position.

4. GETTING GOING

"Try to turn the sudden changes in your life into easy transitions." This small hint was given to me by an older friend and I still try to invoke its message whenever I am faced with some kind of transition. Don't work full time until Friday and retire on Monday. Don't lay out in the sun for six hours after having spent the last six months indoors and never leave your bike untouched in the garage until the first day of your tour. As is the case with many things, bicycle touring also has a universal maxim: "Train hard, tour easy." This is not to say that you'll need to join a gym to get ready for a few weekend tours over the summer, just ride a bit more in your normal routine.

An excellent way to stay in shape for an upcoming tour and limit your share of contributions to global poisoning is to commute to work on your bike. If your place of employment is just too far, try fulfilling your more local transportation needs on your bike. Panniers full of groceries can simulate a touring-size load. Visit cross town friends or spend time with the kids on an afternoon ride. Anything to get used to riding on a daily basis will translate into a much more enjoyable tour.

If these ideas are not for you, you might consider a regular training program in order for you to improve your cardio-pulmonary (heart & lungs) level of fitness. There is a very simple formula which anyone can use to evaluate their level of fitness and monitor improvement. For any real strengthening to occur you must set aside at least 20 minutes three times a week for training. This is a relatively short amount of time to spend considering the benefits you will receive. Not only will you be preparing for your tour but also raising your overall energy level, improving the efficiency of your digestive system, and reducing daily stress. Of course before embarking on any new exercise plan it is best to consult your physician.

The simple formula mentioned above is based on your age and resting heart rate. Begin with the number 220 and subtract your age. This number is your maximum heart rate. You should never actually reach your maximum HR since this could be hazardous. Next step is to determine your resting heart rate. Do this by taking your pulse in the morning before you get out of bed. Locate your pulse at one of two places: on the palm side of your wrist just below the thumb or the carotid arteries on either side of your wind-pipe. Once you have located your pulse look at a clock and count the number of beats within 15 seconds. The first beat should be counted as zero, the second as one and so forth. After you have the total multiply by four. This number is your resting heart rate (HR). Your training range lies between 60% and 80% of the difference between your resting HR and max HR. For example, for a 34 year old with a resting HR of 70 beats per minute to gain cardio-pulmonary fitness he or she would need to elevate their HR to between 140 and 163 beats per minute for 20 minutes at a time, three times per week.

When riding for a conditioning program simply take your pulse at various times along the way and adjust the intensity of your riding to keep your HR in the training range for you. This formula applies for any kind of exercise, but it makes sense to use cycling as your medium if a tour is planned for the future. Begin this program at least six weeks before your planned departure.

It is also important to vary the terrain over which you train. One day work on some sprints, being careful not to punch through the top end of your training range. Another day try some hills. Still another day go for some long, slow distance. You might even try loading your bike down with more weight than you anticipate carrying so that when you actually tour your real load will be pleasantly lighter than your training load. This will eventually give you a wide training profile and prepare you well for anything the road throws at you.

Stretching

Your muscles are the engines on which you will rely for transportation. It makes sense to keep them healthy and a big part of this is stretching before, during and after your daily rides. Stretching helps to removes lactic acids, waste products of respiration, from between muscle fibers. Stretching will also prevent injuries such as pulled or strained muscles, sprains and ligament damage.

Try the following stretches before you get on your bicycle in the morning. Remember that cold muscles should only be stretched lightly. Figure 4-1 depicts some stretches which may work for your pre-ride routine. They can be performed on any flat surface available. I usually pack up all my equipment except for my ensolite pad which I stretch on, then I'm ready to go immediately after stretching. Figure 4-2 shows stretches which can be done while riding. Only try these in a place where traffic is light or nonexistent.

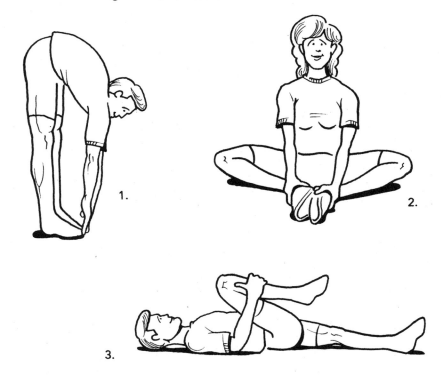

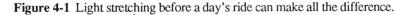

Figure 4-1 Light stretching before a day's ride can make all the difference.

4.

5.

After a day's ride is probably the most important time to stretch in order to rid the muscle fibers of lactic acid (a by-product of muscle activity) and promote the growth of new muscle fiber. Repeat the stretches in Figure 4-1 now and hold them for 30-45 seconds each. Don't forget to massage and shake your muscles loose after a day of riding to remove the lactic acid from between your muscle fibers.

Care of Knees and Feet

Most non-accident related cycling injuries will occur in the knees and feet. All moveable parts break down at one time or another but steps can be taken to prevent this. The primary rule is to know your limits when it comes to distance and level of intensity. If you do not pay careful attention to the signals your feet and legs are sending you, injury could be just around the corner.

Before beginning each day take a few minutes to loosen up your joints. While sitting, raise your feet and point your toes away from you (plantar flexion) then point them back at yourself (dorsi flexion). Now rotate your feet slowly in all directions from the ankles. Stand on the balls of your feet and slowly lower your heels to the ground and back up. Do this several times.

The health of the knee joints while on tour is essential since a small injury with swelling can force you to scrub the remainder of the ride. Therefore it is imperative to minimize the factors which commonly contribute to knee troubles. If you experience any pain while stretching

Figure 4-2 Try some of these stretches while riding.

or warming up you might consider postponing the ride until the source of the pain can be identified. Make sure your saddle height is properly adjusted to its optimum level (see Sizing a Frame, Chapter One). A seat that is too high or too low can cause inflammation in the tendons around the knee cap. Use the gears of your bike to make cycling easy and comfortable. Excessive use of high gears puts too much strain on the knees.

Our first inclination after climbing a big hill is to coast down the other side giving our legs a much deserved rest. Rest, yes, but keep 'em moving! Just standing on your pedals after an uphill drive could cause stiffness in the joints and possibly even an injury when you begin to pump again at the bottom of the hill. Instead, continue to turn the crank, backwards or forward, to prevent stiffening.

5. ON THE ROAD

Keeping yourself alive on our nation's highways is no small concern. An outdoor recreation professor of mine used to say that the most dangerous part of any of our "high adventure" river rafting or rock climbing expeditions was on the highway to and from the point of the activity. And for cyclists that danger is an ever present one if they are sharing the road with motorists. This should not frighten you away from the pursuit, but serve to heighten your level of concern while participating. I have been hit by a car, fortunately at low speed, and it gave me a new perspective on riding in traffic. My basic rule is that one must ride as if one were completely invisible to all motorists. If you follow this rule and master the skills in this chapter you will have a better chance of making it off the road each night in one piece.

Basic Safety

Regardless of one's personal stand on the use of helmets, it can't hurt you to wear one and it can certainly help if you are involved in an accident. A colleague of mine was involved in a very low speed crack-up which resulted in her taking quite a blow to the head. Fortunately, she was wearing a helmet. Yet she still received a serious concussion which resulted in her having to withdraw from classes at the university because her vision and sense of balance had been affected. Her doctor told her that had it not been for the helmet her injuries could have been much more serious, perhaps even fatal.

If you are concerned about your own well being, wear a helmet. If it's more important to feel the wind in your hair and the sun on your scalp then go without, but understand the risk you are taking and make it your own.

Traffic Laws

Never forget that while riding on public roads and highways you are required to follow the same traffic laws as any other driver. This means riding in the right-most lane and using hand signals to inform motorists and fellow riders of your intentions. An indispensable skill which cannot be stressed enough is the glance over the left shoulder to check traffic approaching from the rear before attempting any maneuver. It is vital that you always look before moving to the left for a turn. When making a left-hand turn stay on the right hand side of the turn lane (Figure 5-1) and continue straight into the intersection covering 3/4 of it before actually turning left so as to allow cars plenty of room to pass in the turn.

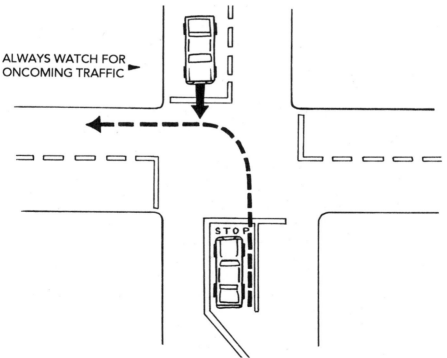

Figure 5-1 Follow this trajectory when hanging a left.

When riding in a group, especially on divided roads with a minimum shoulder clearance it is critical to space riders at least 50 yards apart as a courtesy to drivers who wish to pass. It is far easier to pass a single rider than two, four or more cyclists riding single file along the shoulder.

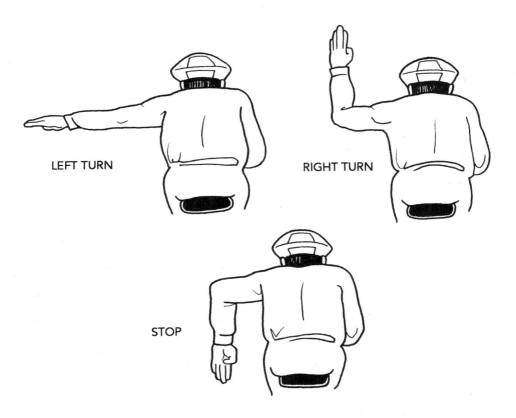

Figure 5-2 Using hand signals in traffic will communicate your intentions to motorists.

It is important to know your hand signals to communicate your intentions to other drivers. Most drivers are happy to share the road with cyclists, but are often caught unawares by what appear to be unpredictable movements in traffic. The use of hand signals will eliminate any confusion between cyclists and motorists. Study the hand signals in Figure 5-2 and get used to using them while riding.

Riding Skills

Riding a bicycle with an extra 40 or 50 pounds sounds like a great effort, but in fact it is not difficult if the load is well packed, properly distributed and tire pressure is adequate. Some would even argue that a loaded bike is easier to ride since added weight provides you with momentum and the feeling of a smooth, long glide. You too may enjoy the "big ride" feeling that accompanies a bike loaded for touring. In any case, follow these simple pointers when negotiating a weighted down bicycle.

- Restrict front panniers to carrying no more than 40% of the total load.

- Always start out in a very low gear when commencing from a dead stop.

- Apply rear brakes initially, then front brakes after a few seconds.

- Don't turn too sharply when maneuvering.

- Small bumps can have a big effect on loaded bike. Take all road profile variations with slow caution. Going over a bump or dip too quickly can mean great stress on the bike and the load.

Cadence

Cadence means the keeping of a pace. It is a law of physics that it takes less energy for an object to maintain a constant speed than it does if one were to vary the speed at different times over the same distance. This is why cars get better mileage on the highway, where speed is more constant, than in city traffic where the speedometer soars and plunges many times over a few miles. This notion of energy conservation holds true for cycling as well.

Any athlete who participates in distance events will tell you the importance of finding and keeping a pace. This allows one to conserve energy and prepare for a strong finish. Finding a pace when you tour will likewise help you to conserve strength to climb that last big hill of the day or cook that elaborate meal once in camp. No one wants to be wiped out after a day's ride, only pleasantly fatigued and anticipating a sound night's sleep. So find a good pace for you and stick to it. Soon your pedaling will become effortless and you'll forget that you are expending any energy at all. At this point you will be free to take in the slowly unrolling scenery and all its treasures that are hidden from the motorists whizzing by at dangerous speeds in their iron coffins.

Shifting

The main reason behind having all those gears is to let you maintain a pace over varied grades or inclines, so use them to your advantage. There are a few pointers to remember when shifting. First, never pedal with any real force while shifting. You should pedal only hard enough to keep the sprockets rolling so the chain can move easily up or down the cluster, or from one chain ring to another. Trying to shift while pumping forcefully, on a hill for example, will cause the chain to jump uncontrollably. This in turn will cause excessive wear of the teeth and, possibly, bury the chain on either side of the free wheel which can be difficult to extract or can even result in damage to the spokes.

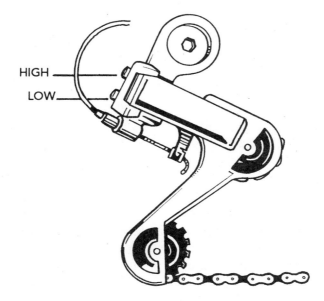

HIGH

LOW

Figure 5-3 Use the adjustment screws to limit the range of your derailleur.

A helpful skill to acquire is the downward and backward "quick glance" between the legs at the freewheel to determine which gear you are in at the moment. Make sure that all is clear ahead for the next few seconds before doing so. This will give you a feel for how lever movement translates to derailleur movement, assuming of course that you are using a friction shifting system.

Both the front and rear derailleurs have two small spring loaded screws each (Figure 5-3) which control their ranges of motion. While the rear wheel is off the ground, turn the crank with your hand and take the bike through all of its gears. If the derailleur takes the chain too far in one direction, tighten the corresponding screw. If it does not go quite far enough leaving one of the extreme sprockets unusable, loosen the screw until the derailleur can achieve all gears.

Pedaling Techniques

Every cyclist has her or his own trick for getting the most out of every turn of the crank. Only time will allow you to find the best technique for you. But in order to find a comfortable style of stomping on the pedals, you need to try new ways and evaluate them according to some basic techniques.

To get started, try what is commonly referred to as "ankling" (Figure 5-4). This way of pedaling will take some concentration at first but will be beneficial since more muscles will be active in each stroke. You will need to have toe clips and straps to successfully execute the ankling technique. Begin at the 12 o'clock position with the toe pointed straight ahead; the foot is flat. At about 3 o'clock the toe should cross the horizontal and be pointing down now with the angle slowly increasing to about 45 degrees by the time you cross the 6 o'clock position. During the upward part of the stroke the toes should be pointed down and the leg should be pulling up as if you were pulling your foot out of a sock. At the 9 o'clock position begin to elevate the toe to be in position for the next down stroke.

If you don't have toe clips on your bike try this "free-foot" technique (Figure 5-4). Begin at 12 o'clock with the toe pointed slightly upward at a 10-15 degree angle. From 12 to about 5 o'clock push down, but slightly forward as well. At the 5 o'clock point the toes downward reversing the angle now to about 20 degrees below the horizontal. Now push backward through the 6 o'clock as if powering off of your back foot when running. This technique will give you a little more umpf out of each stroke.

Experiment with these and any other techniques you discover along the way to come up with your own personal favorite. Then practice whenever you ride to make it an involuntary part of your cycling style.

Hills

One of the most common utterances heard from a novice bicycle tourist is "I'll never make it up that hill!" The truth is that just about any hill can be managed with proper use of your gears. Don't think of a hill climb as an impending period of pure misery, but rather a small physical challenge to be met. And then think of how much fun it will be to zoom down the other side.

Downshift just as you get to the base of the hill so as to maintain cadence. Continue to downshift as the pitch of the incline becomes more steep. Using a small chain ring (28 teeth or less) in combination with the largest sprocket on your freewheel will help you to climb even the steepest monsters.

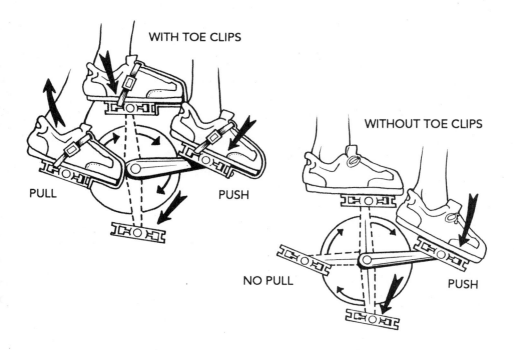

WITH TOE CLIPS

PULL   PUSH

WITHOUT TOE CLIPS

NO PULL   PUSH

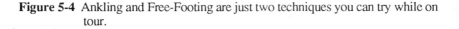

Figure 5-4 Ankling and Free-Footing are just two techniques you can try while on tour.

How to Pack

As we mentioned before, how to pack your bike is just as much a personal style decision as how you decorate your home. Much depends on what you plan on bringing along and how much you plan to use particular items. Take your time and give some serious thought to how you will arrange your baggage. In this section we will consider some general rules for packing that will save you a headache or two along the way. To know the best way to pack for your trip, be sure to read the section entitled "The Shake-Down Ride" (see page 47).

Regardless of the method you use to carry gear on your bike, be it panniers or a duffel bag tied on with rope, it is always a good idea to keep the heavier, more dense items as close to the ground as possible. This will keep your center of gravity low and give you a more stable feeling while riding. If using panniers or a split carrier system of some kind, balance out the heavier items so the weight on each side is relatively equal.

Items which you use more often should be easily accessible. Your wind and rain shell should be ready for donning at a moment's notice. Likewise, your tool kit (see Maintenance and Repair page 57) should be one zipper away from your hands to make minor adjustments without having to disassemble an expert packing job.

With almost any packing configuration there is usually an area on the top of the load which is more or less flat. This relatively level area, what I like to call the deck, is an ideal place to keep those items which are either frequently used or not easily accommodated anywhere else in the pack. With the help of a few bungee cords almost anything can be strapped on deck. I like to keep most of my food on deck in a plastic bag, especially bread or other squishable foodstuffs. In this way I can have a little snack at any time or if I buy some fruit at a roadside stand it can be easily accommodated without a major re-packing effort. Other items which go nicely on deck are maps, laundry or towels that need to dry, guidebooks, sunscreen or even small pets.

The most important thing to remember is to find the packing arrangement that works best for you, even if this means going on an organized group tour where all the essentials are packed for you and driven ahead to the evening's destination.

6. GOOD EATIN'

Nutrition is a key concern of anyone who relies on their body to perform strenuous tasks on a daily basis. Deficiencies in certain nutritional categories, which, under sedentary conditions, might not be noticed, will become pronounced and problematic during periods of high physical activity. In order for your body to respond to the physical demands which you place upon it, your body will demand certain nutrients. Unfortunately, your body does not produce a shopping list of what it wants, it simply ceases to function at optimum levels. If you sit in an office all day you may not notice any such deficiencies, but halfway through a 50 mile ride there will be no mistaking the signs of an insufficient diet. In order to prevent this, you should know a little about basic nutrition and the special daily needs of a cyclist on tour. We will discuss where to find the best kinds of foods as well as some hints for easy preparation and how to assemble a traveling kitchen.

Carbohydrates

These are the chief source of energy for daily activity. Carbohydrates can be divided into three basic categories: complex carbohydrates, double sugars and simple sugars. Complex carbohydrates come from foods like cereals, grains and starches. Since it takes the body a long time to digest complex carbohydrates, they give a cyclist an even, slow burning source of energy throughout the day. Eating plenty of things like granola, oatmeal, breads, potatoes and tortillas will assure an adequate energy supply throughout the day.

Double sugars, like white sugar, white flour and other processed foods should be avoided because they lack the essential minerals and vitamins found in unprocessed whole grains and starches. These sugars also boost the glucose level of the blood to inordinately high levels only to plummet a short while later.

Simple sugars are those found in fruit and honey. These sugars are the easiest for the body to digest and supply you with almost instant energy. If you are feeling the need for a quick boost, reach for some fruit before a candy bar. Diluted fruit juice carried in a water bottle is an ideal way to access extra energy without sending your blood sugar sky high.

Fats

Fats are the most highly concentrated form of energy available to the body. Fats are also needed for proper functioning of the nervous system and production of hormones, as well as being responsible for the transportation of non-water soluble vitamins like A, D, E and K. To insure that you get enough fat in your diet while on the road, take a small plastic bottle of olive oil to use for cooking or as a seasoning for breads or salads.

Proteins

Proteins are the body's building blocks. They are used to repair muscle, hair, skin, tissue and blood vessels. You'll need to get plenty of protein during your tour to reconstruct the tiny muscle fibers which tear on a microscopic level during exercise. Meat and fish are excellent sources of protein as are eggs and soy products. Legumes are almost-complete proteins. When beans are combined with whole grain rice for a meal it makes a protein which rivals meat.

Vitamins and Minerals

All of the essential vitamins and minerals needed by the body must be replenished frequently, especially during periods of high activity. An absence of any of these will cause a slow decrease in efficiency on the cellular level. While this deficiency may be asymptomatic at home, an increase in activity will surely deplete an already low supply of nutrients. For this reason it is recommended that you begin taking a vitamin and mineral supplement with meals about one month before leaving and continue to do so during the tour. This will give your body a chance to re-supply itself, a rather slow process, before you make any extra demands on it.

Water

While food and nutrients are certainly important to a healthy tour, nothing is as critical, yet so often overlooked, as water. All of your body's functions require water in copious amounts. Add to this the physical stress of cycling long distances each day and the minimum amount of water to be consumed doubles. As a general rule drink one liter in the morning before starting out, one liter for every hour of riding and one liter at the end of the day. Dehydration can occur rapidly and result in lethargy, dizziness, fatigue and severe headache.

A Touring Cyclist's Daily Needs

Begin your day by eating some fruit or hot beverages with honey. This will give you the quick energy to get up and running. At the same meal eat some complex carbohydrates to provide you with fuel throughout the morning's ride. Towards mid-day begin to incorporate proteins in your food stops while continuing to eat carbohydrates. This will insure that the proteins are completely absorbed into the blood stream and available for muscle repair overnight. For an evening meal continue with carbohydrates and concentrate on vegetables to provide nutrients and aid digestion. This would also be an ideal time to take a vitamin and mineral supplement.

A Portable Kitchen

Unless you plan on taking all of your meals in restaurants or ready to eat from the grocery store, you'll need to put together a small kitchen that can be carried in one or two ditty bags. With a little ingenuity you can assemble some big luxuries in a very small space. Here's a list of what I carry on tour to assure gastronomic delight.

1 One quart pot w/ lid to heat water, boil pasta, steam veggies, etc.
1 small skillet to sauté, make pancakes, etc.
1 Insulated cup
1 Swiss army knife
1 Pot holder
1 Wooden spatula
1 Frisbee as a plate, cutting board & toy

1 Combo salt & pepper shaker
1 6 oz. squeeze bottle of olive oil
1 Head garlic
4 small plastic spice containers (oregano, dill, basil & tarragon)
2 Sets silverware
1 Set chopsticks
1 Plastic coffee cone & cloth filter
1 Collapsible water carrier (2.5 gallons)

This list has worked well for me but may not completely satisfy your own needs. That's why it is important to go on a shake-down ride (see page 47) before embarking on a multi-day tour. Only after cooking with a portable kitchen will you get a feel for what may be missing.

Stoves on Wheels

There are a myriad of compact, lightweight camping stoves on the market today each with their own advantages and shortcomings. Space limitations prohibit us from discussing each of them here. Check the back issues of the popular outdoor magazines for a recent review of the

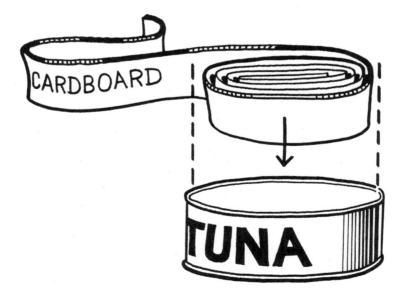

Figure 6-1 A modified tuna can makes a great camp stove cartridge.

available models. Another option is to visit a few different sporting goods stores, tell them what you'll be doing and how much you have to spend. Don't buy until you have checked at least three establishments to get an objective idea of what your money can buy.

If you are not planning on doing much cooking and would never use a camping stove for any other outdoor pursuits, you may want to consider making your own stove out of inexpensive household materials. All you need is an empty tuna fish can, some corrugated cardboard and paraffin wax. Cut the cardboard into a strip about 2 feet long. The width should match the height of the tuna can. Roll the strip up tightly and place it in the can (Figure 6-1). Now melt the wax in a pan and pour it into the tuna can making sure that all of the long spaces in the cardboard have been filled. Once cooled, you have a short, wide candle which can generate quite a bit of heat. Slide the lid over the top to control the flame. Use three rocks or some other means to cradle the pot over the flame. When finished cooking simply blow out the flame and allow to cool before packing.

Spoke Bending Recipes

Try the following super easy dishes on the shake-down ride or at some point during the tour. They are made to be improved upon and personalized. If you come up with a particularly good twist to any of the following or have invented a favorite touring recipe of your own, send it in to me, care of the publisher, and we'll print the best savories in the next edition.

Pedaler's Porridge

1/3 cup rolled oats per person (about one large handful)
2/3 cup water per person
2 tablespoons peanut butter
1/3-1/2 cup dried fruit, diced (apricots, prunes, apples, pineapples and raisins)
1 fresh banana sliced

Bring water to a boil, add oats and stir occasionally for one minute. Remove from stove and stir in the dried fruit and peanut butter. Cover and set aside for two minutes. Garnish with banana slices.

Penne tutto mare

1 tablespoon olive oil
1 small onion, diced
3 cloves garlic, germ removed, pressed or chopped
2/3 cup penne pasta per person (or substitute pasta)
2 tablespoons tomato paste
8 oz. selected seafood (canned anchovies, crab, sardines or shrimp)

Boil pasta in plenty of water for five minutes. Remove, cover and wrap pot in towel. Set aside for ten minutes. Sauté onion and garlic in the olive oil. After a few minutes add the seafood with juices. Add tomato paste and stir together. Drain pasta and pour seafood over.

Power Pita

1 piece round pita bread
4 slices of cheese
1 tomato, sliced
6 slices of salami
2 leaves of lettuce or tufts of sprouts
1 tablespoon of mustard or other topping

Tear the pita in half and stuff each half with ingredients mentioned above. Include any other favorites like olives or capers.

In addition to the ingredients mentioned above there are those staple foods like dry soup mixes, flat breads, popcorn or rice cakes, hard cheeses, tea, beef jerky, fruit leather, trail mix, ginger snaps, bagels and peanut butter which travel well under the most arduous conditions. Add to this incomplete list any items which are light, do not require refrigeration, and will not spoil quickly.

7. PLANNING A TRIP

In the preceding chapters we have discussed almost everything, save maintenance and repair, that you need to be concerned with while on a bike tour. But how do you plan for one? How do you decide where to go? What time of year? Where to stay along the way? Again, only you know what's best for you. There are a few things to consider when choosing a route that we will examine in this chapter but the final choice as to the type of route is up to you. The brand of cycling which you prefer will probably dictate more than any other factor where you go the first time, but don't limit your horizons to one kind of touring. Try as many different trips as possible during your touring career. Perhaps you will pioneer a new way of living on a bicycle.

The Joy of Living on a Bicycle

Whether it be cycling from chateau to Champagne cellar in France or tracing the Mormon trail from Missouri to Utah, there is a singular, intrinsic sense of pure contentment that is derived from propelling yourself and all items necessary for a comfortable existence down a road at your own pace and to your own schedule. Nothing else, in my mind, compares to the freedom of having empty days in front of you to fill with riding in any direction you please.

If this seems like platitudinous puff to you right now you're not alone. A Dutch woman I met once while touring in Africa told me that her first bike trip was "no fun at all. Lots of rain and bad food." For some reason she went again another time, probably, she said "because I knew it seemed like it could be fun. Deep down I knew that." Today she rents out her house in the Netherlands and spends most of her time cycling different parts of the world. She lives to tour!

You are bound to run into people like this at some point during your touring career. You may even become a person like this in which case you will preach the bicycle touring gospel with every pump of the pedals. Or, you may feel like my Dutch friend did after her first tour and not want to continue. The point is that living on a bicycle, just like anything else in life, is an art. A person will only become an artist of anything after searching for a form and style of his or her own. If you can make living on a bicycle one of your forms it will provide you with an endless means of self discovery and personal enrichment, not to mention excitement, adventure, independent travel and healthy exercise. And remember the most important point of all: it's supposed to be fun.

Route Selection

If you can ride a bike over it, you can tour it. There are no limits to where one can go, only self-imposed parameters of terrain characteristics, daily distance, amount of food and water to be carried and so forth. It is probably wise, though, to start with a route that has an intensive ground support system in place. By this I mean a route which has numerous places to replenish food supplies along the way, easy access to water, telephones, and suitable places to spend the night. Once you become adept at living on a bike, you can select routes which take you farther from such conveniences.

Many of us forget that some of the best places to tour are right in our own back yard. There is a plethora of secondary roads in the United States that have been forgotten since the introduction of super highways. Any detailed map of your area will show these secondary roads, or blue highways, which make for ideal touring routes since traffic is often light and scenery abounds. By using such highways in your immediate area, you can begin your tour from home and end at home, eliminating the need to drive to a starting point of a more popular route.

If touring a piece of local territory or planning your own route from a map is not appealing to you, there are many guide books on the market (see appendix D) for directing you through many diverse and exciting places by bicycle. These detailed guides will typically include mileage logs, points of interest, services, and alternative routes all along the way. These guides are quite helpful if you plan to hit the ground riding because you can read all about what you are going to experience before you even start. Many sporting goods stores and bike shops will carry a number of titles on the subject.

Where to Sleep?

The question of nightly accommodations is most likely a question of financial resources. Staying in a hotel each night or a cozy little bed & breakfast is a splendid way to tour, if you can afford it. But even if you have the extra cash, you may find it more pleasing and more rewarding on a personal level to camp out. There are a number of different options available to the touring cyclist that we shall look at briefly.

International Youth Hostels, of which there are many around the more popular tourist regions in the US, are usually clean, if rustic, and always affordable. You need not be "young" as the name implies to stay at a Youth Hostel, only be a card-carrying member of the IYH Federation. If you are not a member, you can usually join on the spot for a nominal fee.

Organized campgrounds are excellent spots to pass the evening and are usually very inexpensive for those of us not arriving in motor vehicles. In many public campgrounds there are designated hiker/biker campsites located away from the car campers. These sites typically cost three to four times less per night than a regular car camping site. If there are no designated hiker/biker sites available, you will probably be directed to the day use area with the stipulation that you are on the road by a certain time in the morning.

A person on a bicycle tour is a particularly non-threatening element. For this reason people along the way will approach you and ask questions about where you are going, for how long, etc. Don't be afraid to do the same. I often stop at rural residences in the late afternoon to ask if I might camp somewhere on their property for one night making it clear that I will be leaving the next morning. I have never been turned away. In fact, many times I've been invited into the house for dinner and treated like a member of the family.

One of the key advantages to being on your bike is that you can easily fade into a landscape without being noticed by anyone.

Exploring unpopulated areas can yield first class accommodations for free. Some of the most beautiful campsites I have ever had the pleasure of using were discovered in this way. Finding these forgotten, in-between places is an art. With time you will learn to pick your entry points carefully (Figure 7-1). Make sure to have enough food and water for the night before you start to explore. Begin looking for small dirt roads or trails which break off from the main route in the afternoon. Respect all 'no trespassing' and 'private property' signs. Unmarked paths, however, are fair game. Explore a few of these uncontrolled easements for suitable sleeping areas. If you find a place that's "okay" but not perfect, go on down the road a little more until you find the perfect site. If it gets too late before you find the ideal spot, you can always go back to the "okay" spot. Observe the rules of minimum impact camping while in these areas: no campfires, carry out all trash and leave no evidence that you were ever there. It is also a good idea to do all your cooking before dark so as not to attract any unwanted attention.

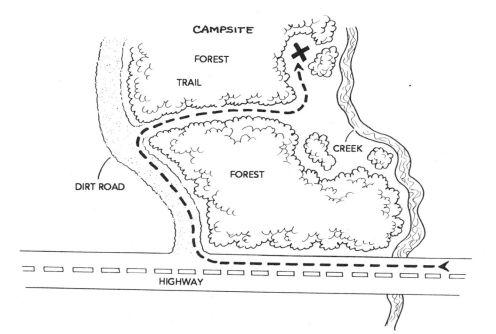

Figure 7-1 An example of how to find an informal campsite for the night.

The Shake-Down Ride

If you have never been on a tour before you should initiate yourself the easy way, by taking a one night practice run somewhere close to home. The reasons for this are threefold. First, it gives you a chance to practice all of the requisite skills of a cycling tourist without the pressure of having to worry about actually getting anywhere. Secondly, you will have a chance to forget a needed item without paying the price of doing without it for the whole tour. Thirdly, it will give you the confidence of knowing the best way to pack, set-up and use your equipment before you begin a real multi-day tour. And instead of being anxious throughout the first day's ride, which can be pretty demanding in itself, you can relax and enjoy the scenery and think, "I've done this before. I know what to expect."

Choose a destination anywhere between five and twenty miles of your home. It could be a local park, campground or even a friend's house across town. Pack everything just as you would if you were going on a long distance, multi-day tour (except for food; bring one to two day's worth or buy en route). Bring along a small pad and pencil to take notes on things to do differently and what else to take or leave at home for the next trip.

Set up camp and make an evening meal just as you would if you were on that big tour. Use your stove as much as possible during this field test, but keep track of cooking time. Then, when the stove is cool, check fuel consumption to get an idea of how long the stove will run on a particular unit of fuel. Even if the sky is clear and the weather warm, pitch your tent or other means of shelter, take it down and pitch it again. It may seem silly, but this practice could prove indispensable if you ever have to pitch your tent after dark.

In the morning make some hot beverages, pack up and ride home. Even though you've only been gone one night, it will seem like a long, relaxing weekend. What's more, you'll be ready for a longer tour at just a few hours notice because now you know what goes into a multi-day tour: the same things that it took to make your shake-down ride a success, only more food!

8. MAINTENANCE AND REPAIR

Bicycles are very durable machines. They can withstand a great deal of punishment and still function at or near optimum operational levels. And with a little preventative maintenance, there is no reason why your machine should not be able to roll on for a lifetime. To insure that you steer clear of mechanical problems it is important to lubricate regularly and clean the bike often. This chapter will not make you a bicycle mechanic, but it will enable you to identify problems and do something about them before they become debilitating ones. This chapter will also help you understand how to undertake simple repairs on your own in the field.

Regular Lubrication

There is a clear incentive for keeping the moving parts of your bicycle, especially the chain, well lubricated. Well lubed parts make pedaling much easier. You will also extend the life of your chain and all other moving parts through regular lubrication. I say lubrication and not grease because the use of a petroleum product will mean attracting dirt to the lubricated part. Instead, use a silicone lubricant which will perform the same for a longer period of time without being a sticky depository for dust and dirt. Tri-Flo® is a brand I recommend.

Use the silicone lubricant (make sure you don't get silicone sealer) on any and all moving parts except the wheel hubs . Give a little squirt to the derailleurs, brake calipers (not the pads), shift levers and even the pedal spindles. If you are covering 40-50 miles per day or more, you may want to lubricate the chain each morning before starting out, possibly even during the day depending on the weather conditions. Hot, dry, dusty conditions will tend to break down silicone more rapidly.

How to Check for Problems Before they are Problems

Knowing your machine is the first step in being able to trouble shoot for potential breakdowns. The only way to know your machine is to spend time with it. This is another good reason for beginning a training regimen before any planned departure. Riding regularly over a wide variety of terrain will familiarize you with all the quirks of your bike. In the garage, spend some time following the cables to their destinations; brakes and derailleurs. Take note of where the sharpest

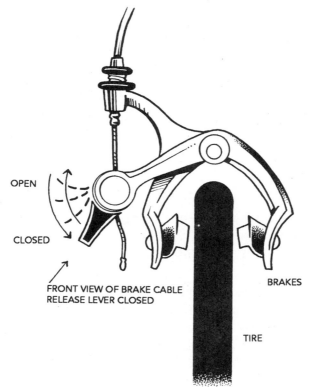

OPEN

CLOSED

FRONT VIEW OF BRAKE CABLE
RELEASE LEVER CLOSED

BRAKES

TIRE

Figure 8-1 Be certain that the cable release lever is in the closed position before riding.

turns occur since this is where the cables are most likely to wear. Observe how the cable release lever on the brakes, used for removing a wheel without having to disconnect the brake cable, (Figure 8-1) affects the feel in the hand set. Wiggle the brake pads to make certain they are secured to the calipers.

If you have quick release hubs (Figure 8-2) be certain which direction is closed and which is open. When in the closed position, keep the quick release levers swept back, parallel to the ground. Pick up the frame and push down on the wheels to make sure they are secured to the frame. Straddle the front wheel to hold it in place and attempt to turn the handle bars from side to side to check for a loose goose neck. This can be tightened by the allen wrench fitting at the top of the gooseneck just before it angles forward.

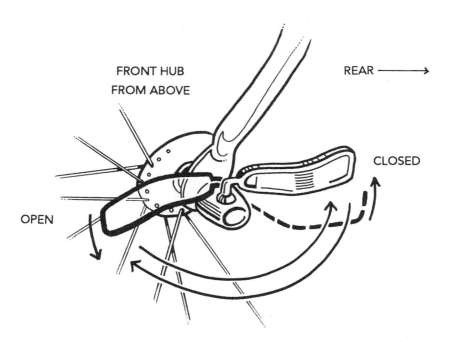

Figure 8-2 Quick release hubs make for easy wheel removal.

Check the alignment of your wheels often by looking directly down on them. The distance between the side wall of the tire and the frame should be equal for both sides. Pluck each spoke lightly like playing a harp to check for broken ones. All should have about the same tone or pitch. An unusually high pitch means a spoke is over stressed (see out-of-true rims page 54).

Inspect all nuts and bolts periodically. Losing a bolt while on the road can range from being a little annoying to completely debilitating depending on what you loose. The bolts which hold racks to the frame are always coming loose due to the weight constantly shifting while riding.

Keep an eye on the pattern of wear on your tires. Heavy loads will wear out tires rapidly. The rear tire will always wear down before the front. It might be a good idea to rotate the tires to extend their combined overall life span.

Repairs

You need not have ever done a bicycle repair before in your life to complete the following fix-it jobs. These will be the most common problems you will encounter while on the road. If you feel incompetent with a wrench in your hand and would prefer to give the job to a trained professional, along with a lot of cash, that's up to you. But the simple truth is that you seldom break down next to a bike shop. You should know how to do some of the simplest tasks on your own. And who knows, you may end up discovering a new hobby.

Flats

Getting a flat tire is an unavoidable part of cycling. It is especially annoying while on tour since it usually means having to unload the bike in order to remove the wheel to fix the puncture. You can either get upset and try to rush through the job, or shrug it off and enjoy the time it takes to do a good job. Think of it as an inevitable part of touring. If, however, it is critical that you move on quickly, just change inner tubes and forget about repairing the leak. This option requires that you carry a spare tube with you at all times.

In either case, begin by removing the wheel and completely deflating the tube. Then take a tire iron (Figure 8-3) and slip it between the side wall of the tire and the inside edge of the rim, concave side up. Pry out the base of the tire using the rim as a fulcrum and hook the opposite end of the iron around the closest spoke. Take the second tire

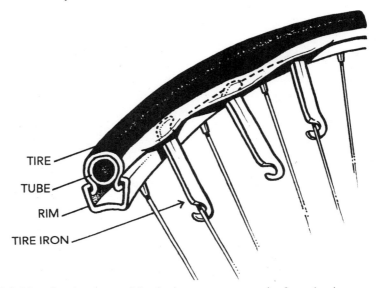

TIRE

TUBE

RIM

TIRE IRON

Figure 8-3 Note the placement of the tire irons to remove a tire from the rim.

iron and insert it in the same fashion two to three inches from the first. At this point a sufficient amount of the tire should be outside the rim to allow you to pry out the rest of the tire in five to six inch sections. After you have gone around the entire circumference, you are still left with half of the tire on the rim. Simply repeat the first part of the process to lift the other half off.

Now that you have the tube and the tire separated from the wheel, take the tube out of the tire and re-inflate it. Locate the leak(s) by listening and feeling for escaping air or convey the tube through a few inches of water. Mark all punctures with a pen, chalk or by scratching lightly on the tube itself. Cover an area just larger than the size of the patch with rubber cement. Allow to dry before adhering the patch to the tube. When you do apply the patch, be sure to press from the center outwards to avoid air bubbles.

When you are confident that all leaks have been sealed, deflate the tube completely, place inside the tire and guide the stem through the hole in the rim. Refit the tire over the rim one side at a time by hand. If it becomes difficult to do so, use a tire iron hooking the concave side over the edge of the rim and pry the tire into place. IMPORTANT NOTE: Do not allow any part of the tube to be pinched between the tire and the rim while remounting the tire. This could result in another puncture.

Out-of-True Rims

Perfectly true rims are a rare commodity. A shining aluminum band that neither sways from side to side when spinning nor rises and falls on the vertical are rare indeed. But after several days of loaded touring and a few driveways taken a little too quickly this exemplary bit of velo engineering that appeared to have been crafted in zero gravity will look like an oscillating hula hoop. Of course I'm exaggerating, but rims tend to work themselves out-of-true more often than most of us think they should. Unfortunately, truing a rim is a delicate operation, an art form really, that even many experienced bicycle mechanics will admit they have not yet perfected. However, the theory behind truing a rim is rather simple, putting it into practice is the hard part. If you are going to attempt truing a rim, give yourself plenty of time and a decent work space.

With the bike upside-down, preferably with the tire and tube off, remount the rim, spin it and watch for the repeating pattern of the deformity. Let the rim slow down and pinpoint the highest or most profound spot in the deformity. For example, if the rim is swaying to the left then coming back to center, find the point at which the rim comes closest to the left brake pad. Mark this spot on the rim with a felt pen, chalk or a small piece of tape. Now locate the two spokes on either side of this point which anchor on the left side of the hub. Do the same for the two spokes on each side of the high point which are anchored on the right side of the hub. Essentially all you will do is loosen the spokes that are on the same side as the high point and tighten the spokes on the opposite side. But do so in very small increments: 1/8 to 1/4 of a turn for each. Then spin the rim again and check the results. IMPORTANT NOTE: The spoke nipples appear to have reverse threads but just think of it as if you were tightening or loosening a nut up and down an inverted bolt.

Broken Spokes

Spokes will tend to break while touring due to the increased load. That's why it is important to know what size spokes each of your wheels take. Have a few extra with you on tour. You can buy them at any bike store and carry them taped to your frame or your rack.

Spokes tend to break most often on the rear wheel and, if you're really unlucky, on the freewheel side of the hub. This is an extra pain since it usually means having to remove the freewheel to replace the spoke. For this you will need a special freewheel nut made to fit your particular freewheel. Once the tire and tube are off (and freewheel removed if necessary) unscrew the nipple completely and remove any fragments from the spoke hole in the hub. Thread the new spoke through the hub and the rim. Check the other spoke arrangements and follow suit. Screw down the nipple to the approximate position and check for true.

You may want to purchase an emergency spoke which is simply an adjustable length of cable with the appropriate hooks on either end to quickly replace a broken spoke. With this kind of device there is no need to worry about a lengthy procedure on the roadside, especially if it's getting towards sunset. Just throw on the emergency spoke and continue your ride until you find a more suitable time and place to attempt a spoke replacement.

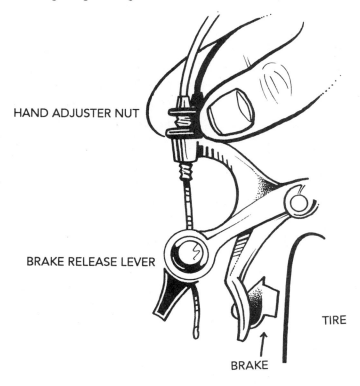

HAND ADJUSTER NUT

BRAKE RELEASE LEVER

TIRE

BRAKE

Figure 8-4 Use the brake cable adjuster nut to make your brakes responsive and safe.

Brake Adjustment and Pad Replacement

You will be able to tell when your brakes need adjusting by the feel in the hand brake lever. The more you need to squeeze the more your brakes need adjusting. A good general rule is that once the hand lever passes the halfway point between the open position and the handlebar it's time to adjust. This can be done in a few different ways depending on your braking system. In most cases there is a threaded, metal tube called the cable adjuster housing through which the brake cable passes. This is located either above the hand lever or where the cable leaves the sheath just before connecting with the calipers. To adjust the brakes, simply screw this tube in or out from its mounting (Figure 8-4). Then screw the adjuster nut, which is around the housing itself, down against the mounting to hold fast the new position. If this is not a feature on your bike then you will have to adjust where the brake cable is attached to the pull arm of the brake calipers. Do this by loosening the nut on the pull arm and draw a small amount of cable through the hole, re-tightening the bolt at a spot just above the old crimp point.

To replace the brake pads just remove the nut on the back of the pad. Take note of where the old pad was located in the long, oval slot of the caliper and replace the new one in the same position. Once the new pads are in place, clinch the brakes to make certain that all of the surface of the pad comes into contact with the rim.

Broken Cables and Chains

If you happen to snap a derailleur or brake cable while on tour there's not much to worry about as long as you have a replacement cable. Get the longest one you could possibly use so that it can be modified down to fit any of the other spots. Never cut excess, just coil up any extra past the crimp point. This way if a longer cable ever breaks you might be able to swap the newly broken one for the original, maximum length replacement cable, the excess of which was wisely coiled up and saved.

A chain break is as easy to remedy and you don't need to carry a replacement chain, just a small tool called a chain rivet extractor. This tool is basically the reverse of a corkscrew in that it forces one of the horizontal rivets through the holes in the sides of the figure eight plates. Simply splice out the faulty section of chain and reconnect. However, if you plan on reconnecting the joint, do not drive the rivet completely free of the outside plate, just enough to free the interior plate.

Tools

The following is a list of tools you should carry with you while touring. All of the following should be able to fit in a small bag weighing between two and three pounds. If you ever run into a mechanical problem that you are not sure about, don't panic. You will, if you carry all of these items, have the tools to do a wide variety of repairs. Just reason out what you need to do or what will work temporarily until you can get to a repair shop. You would be surprised at what many people in this world use to repair their bikes. Be creative and use all of your resources to remedy the problem.

Crescent wrench

Tri star socket wrenches
   (2-12mm)

Small pair of vice grips

Small screwdrivers:
   phillips & standard

Spare spokes (taped to frame
   or rack)

Valve core extractor

Set of allen wrenches

Tire repair kit

3 tire irons

Spoke wrench

Freewheel remover

2 long cables

2 small hose clamps for
   temporary repairs of racks, etc.

Appendix A

EQUIPMENT CHECK LIST

Clothing
lycra cycling shorts
2 short sleeve t-shirts
walking shorts
neck-to-ankle inner layer (polypropylene or cotton)
insulating layer (sweats, fleece or natural wool)
shell outer layer
cycling shoes
casual shoe/sandals
sunglasses
riding gloves

Shelter
tarp w/lots of cord or a tent
sleeping bag or blankets
sleeping pad
sheet or bag liner

Cooking Gear
stove
one quart pot w/lid
sauce pan
insulated cup

pot holder
wooden spatula
Frisbee
salt & pepper
olive oil
spices
plastic silverware
chopsticks
coffee making paraphernalia
large capacity water container

Personal Items
toiletries
all purpose liquid soap (Dr. Bronner's is excellent)
sunscreen
lip balm
flashlight
lightweight towel
maps
first-aid kit
insect repellent

For the Bike
water bottle
bike light
lock
bungee cords
pump
repair kit (see chapter 7)

Extras
radio
book
pad & pen
stamps
camera

Appendix B

MAIL ORDER COMPANIES

Basic Designs (Insulated sleeping pads)
5815 Bennett Valley Road
Santa Rosa, CA 95404

California Best (Footwear and activewear)
800/CAL-BEST
Department 3022

Campmor (General outdoor clothing & equipment)
PO Box 998-6A
Paramous, NJ 07633
201/445-5000

Leisure Outlet (Discount camping equipment)
421 Soquel Avenue
Santa Cruz, CA 95062
800/332-1460

Feathered Friends (Mainly down bags & outerwear)
2013 4th Avenue
Department O
Seattle WA, 98121
206/441-8229

L.L. Bean (The perrenial favorite)
Casco Street
Freeport, ME 04033

Lowe Alpine Systems (Outdoor clothing)
PO Box 1449
Broomfield, CO 80038

Moonstone (Outerwear, extreme weather)
5350 Ericson Way
Arcata, CA 95521
707/822-2985

Patagonia Mail Order (Smart outdoor wear - aka:Patagucci)
PO Box 8900
Department 30736H
Bozeman, MT 59715
800/336-9090

REI (Complete line of outdoor products including panniers)
Department N2134
Sumner, WA 98352-0001
800/426-4840

Sierra Trading Post (Discount Mail-order outlet)
5025 Campstool Road
Department OU1092
Cheyenne, WY 82007
307/775-8000

Sequel (Outdoor clothing)
PO Box 3185
Department O
Durango, CO 81302
303/385-4660

Appendix C

CYCLING PERIODICALS

Bicycling
33 East Minor Street
Emmaus, PA 18098
215/967-5171
10 issue/yr. $19.97

Bicycle Guide
711 Boylston Street
Boston, MA 02116
617/236-1885
9 issue/yr. $14.90

California Bicyclist
490 2nd Street #304
San Francisco, CA 94107
415/546-7291
12 issues/yr. $30

Cycling USA (Official publication of the United States Cycling
         Federation)
1750 East Boulder Street
Colorado Springs, CO 80909
719/578-4581
12 issues/yr. $10

Appendix D

TOURING GUIDES

Alley, Jean & Hartley. *Colorado Cycling Guide,* Pruet Publishing: 1989.

Bernotas, Adophe. *Thirty Bicycle Tours in New Hampshire,* Backcountry Publications: 1991.

Boyce, Chris. *North Carolina Biking Guide,* Affordable Adventures; 1989.

Braun, Randall Gray. *Cyclists' Route Atlas: A guide to the Gold Country & High Sierra,* Heyday Books, Berkeley, CA: 1987.

Crow-Hiendlmayr, Jackalene. *The Florida Bicycle Book,* Pineapple Press: 1990.

Emmery, Lena & Susan Taylor. *Grape Expedition in California: 15 Tours across the California Wine Country,* S. Taylor & Friends, San Francisco: 1987.

Hawkins, Karen & Gary. *Bicycle Touring in the western United States,* Pantheon Books, New York: 1982.

Jackson, Joan. *Biking Holidays: 50 Scenic routes to pedal from old Monterey to the Golden Gate*, Valley Publishers: 1981.

Kirkendall, Tom & Vicky Spring. *Bicycling the Pacific Coast*, Mountaineers, Seattle: 1984.

Kugler, B. Kim. *Hudson Valley Bicycle Tours*, Emjay Publishing Company: 1989.

Mullen, Edwin & Jane Griffith. *Short Bike Rides on Cape Cod, Nantucket and the Vineyard*, Globe Pequot: 1991.

Thomas, Paul. *The Best Bike Rides in New England*, Globe Pequot: 1990.

Vanderboom, Gretchen, ed. *Minnesota Biking Guide*, Affordable Adventures: 1989.

APPENDIX E

REPAIR MANUALS

Burstyn, Ben. *Bicycle Repair and Maintenance*. Arco: 1974.

Cuthbertson, Tom. *Anybody's Bike Book*. Ten Speed Press, Berkeley, CA: 1984.

Sloane, Eugene A. *Eugene A. Sloane's Bicycle Maintenance Manual*. Simon & Schuster, New York: 1981.

INDEX

adjustment screws, 34
attire, riding, 21
bottle cages, 13
bungee cords, 12, 36
brakes
    adjustment of, 56
    calipers, 9, 56
    cantilever, 8
    release levers, 50
    shoes for, 9, 56
cadence, 32
campsites, 45
carbohydrates, 37-38
chains, 8, 56
clothing, 19-20, 59
computers, 15
derailleurs, 8, 33, 34
ensolite pads, 19, 27
fats, 38
feet, care of, 27
fenders, 13

flat tires, 52
frames
    configuration, 5
    selection of, 5
freewheel, 2, 54
gears
    description of, 8
    use of, 33, 35
generators, 16
guide books, 44, 45, 65
handlebars, 9
headlights, 16
heart rate, 24
hills, 35
index shifting, 8
inner tubes
    repair of, 52
    selection of, 7
kitchenware, 39-40
knees, care of, 27-28
lactic acid, 27

layering, theory of, 19
luggage racks, 11
lubrication, 49
luxuries, 15
lycra, 20
maintenance, 49-52
minerals, 38
mountain bicycles
    uses for, 3-5
nutrition, 37, 39
packing, 21,36
panniers, 8, 12, 23, 32, 36
pedaling, 22, 34
physical training, 23-34
proteins, 38
rain gear, 20-21
rat traps, (*see* toe clips)
recipes, 41-42
repairs, 52
riding skills, 32
rims, 6, 54
saddles, 9
safety, 29
shake-down ride, 47
shelter, 17
shifting, 8, 33
shoes, 21
shorts, riding, 21
sleeping
    bags, 19
    places for, 45-46
    systems, 18-19

spokes
    damage of, 33
    emergency, 55
    for touring, 6
    maintenance check of, 52
    repair of, 54-55
    tandem arrangement, 6
sprockets, 8, 33
stoves, 40-41
stretching, 26
tarps, 17
tents, 18
tires
    selection of, 7
toe clips, 22
tools, 57
touring
    route selection, 44
    the joy of, 4, 43
touring bicycles
    uses for, 2-3
traffic, riding in, 29-31
trailers, 15
valves, 7
vitamins, 38
walkie-talkies, 16
water, 39